Library of Congress Control Number: 2008910083
ISBN: Softcover   978-1-4363-8447-6

To order additional copies of this book, contact:
Xlibris Corporation
1-888-795-4274
www.Xlibris.com
Orders@Xlibris.com
54437

NOV 2009

'Women', get out of the Domestic Violence Relationship

Willie Bell Ratliff

FORWARD

This book is dedicated to all those who are suffering in domestic violence relationships. It is my desire to help others escape the chains that keep them bound in horrible circumstances. I want other women to see their way free as I did. It took great support from those who were close to me and loved me to achieve my freedom from violence. Now, I want to be part of a support system for others who may not have close family members to help them.

It is also dedicated to those loving family members and friends who were so instrumental in helping me get out of my situation. They continue to help me try to achieve my goals in life. Without them, I would never have been able to write this book.

This started out with a nice young lady that had everything going for her. She met this older man and didn't realize he was an alcoholic. She begins to date this man. Then he slowly began to change. He always had a temper. His attitude was terrible. His friends told her to stay away from this man because he was abusive to women. She wouldn't listen to her friends. She told her friends that she wanted to find him out herself. One day he came home, she smelled alcohol on his breath, and she looked at his eyes and they were red. They got into an argument and she asked him, "Have you been drinking?" He replied, "No." She told him, "Yes you have been drinking." He got very angry with her. He began to change into another person. He pulled his knife out, and he pointed the knife toward her neck. He came very close to her and got in her face and knocked her down on the floor. She blacked out for less than 15 minutes.

He fell down on the floor and he begins to cry out and call her name, "Bell, Bell." He was telling her that he was sorry and he didn't know what happened. He left and went home. She saw an expression on his face that looked like a demon just came out into another person. This man was very, very jealous of her. He was so jealous of her that she couldn't speak to another young man. If she would speak to another man, he would accuse her of being with that man. When she got home, he would start to abuse her and fight her. He also told her that if they kept arguing, one day he is going to take her head and beat it on the door until her daughter would not know who she is. The young lady was so afraid of him she didn't want to tell anybody how she felt. She kept that to herself. She made appointments to go to counseling. She talked to a counselor about her problems. They told her to get out of that relationship. Every time she would go to counseling she would cry and cry. The people would talk to her and ask her what was she going to do about it. She would tell them that she didn't know because she really liked him. One day she went to the mall and asked him to go with her. They got into an argument and argued all the way to the mall. He cursed her out and told her to stop the car. As she stopped the car he told her that he was going to beat her up. He pulled her out of the car and pulled her hair out in the top of her head. She ran into the mall. She saw a lady in the customer services department and told the lady to call the police. However, the lady in the customer services department told her that she didn't have a police in the mall. She told her that she would call the mall security. A couple minutes later the guard came. She began to tell the guard what this man did to her. The guard went to the man and talked with him. She told him that he was being abusive to her, and he could go to jail. She also told him that the best thing for him to do is to get on the bus and go home. The man did exactly what she said. The guard told the young lady to go home. The young lady went home. She called up her daughter and she told her daughter how she was abused at the mall. Later her daughter came over to her house, and she showed her daughter all the bruises on her back and shoulder. Her daughter told her to leave him alone and stay away from him. Later that day, this man called Bell on the phone. Bell's oldest daughter wouldn't let her talk to him over the phone. She told him that if he wouldn't stay away from her mother she would report him to the police. Bell's daughter said a lot of abusive words to him. He told her daughter that he was very sorry for what he had done. Bell eventually stopped being mad at him. Bell did give in and talked to him on the phone. David asked her to forgive him, and Bell said that she would. The young lady kept on going to counseling and had to get on medication for her nerves. She would go into a deep depression when she thought about how he treated her. She would not eat and she lost her self-esteem. Her friends and her daughters couldn't understand why she would date an alcoholic and be in an abusive relationship. They all asked her, "How could you." When they asked her that question, she would cry and cry. She told them that she was very afraid of him because alcoholics are very dangerous and they have different personalities. She also told them she wouldn't fight him back because he was somebody else when he got angry. However, he would keep on abusing her.

Alcoholics are very dangerous people. They want to feel like they have control over you. If you don't do what they ask you to do they will hurt you. They have a disease and want to control you and your life. They fight to get what they want. They are very dangerous to be around. Often times they will pick fights with you just to abuse you. Please don't try to fight them back because you will not win. I was told to never fight an alcoholic back because they will hurt you. There are memories of so much pain in my life. My story is very sad and abusive. I want to express how I felt being in an abusive relationship. I lost my self-esteem in dating. I didn't have any respect for myself. I let my family down. I have two daughters, and I failed in everything in my life due to an abusive man. Trust me my story is very painful and sad. When I am alone, I think about him abusing me. The physical and mental abuse is still in my deep memory. I find myself daydreaming about how I was treated. I sit around and read so many books about domestic violence and abuse to women. I think about how I was abused. I would like to date again but I am afraid to date because I feel like another man would be like the last man. I have grown up now, and I have come to realize that I was young and foolish. I was a very loving woman looking for love. I couldn't find it so I went to an alcoholic for love. I felt like I needed attention, comfort and protection. I needed someone to be there for me. My ideas of love were, of course, all wrong. I made a bad decision. When I started dating an alcoholic, my two girls couldn't understand me. My youngest daughter really didn't want me dating him. She asked me,

"What do you see in him?" She also told me, "You're supposed to leave those type of people alone because they are possessed by the devil and they are very dangerous to be around." My oldest daughter was very surprised at me. She told me, "Mama, I am so surprised of you." The only thing that could come out of her mouth was, "Mama, what is wrong with you?" I was so ashamed of myself because I lost my self-esteem. I was more lost than ever. I was so scared. I took my anger out on my children. It was very hard for me to tell my sister. I have two sisters who are ministers. They really love me and they stuck by my side. My daughters were so surprised at me that they told me they were going to call my sisters and tell them about me. I was so afraid of David because I thought if I told he will find out, and give me a good beating. I really hurt my children. I felt weak and worried about my salvation. As time proceeded, I finally had the nerve to tell my sisters. I had to learn not to feel. I'm sure you all understand how I felt. I was alone, and as time passed by, I went into depression. I wanted to move into another house because I would see his spirit in my house. I wanted to buy new furniture for my house. I just wanted to change everything. I lost my self-esteem so badly that I thought I couldn't help myself. I couldn't get along with my two daughters. My oldest daughter and I would argue all the time. My oldest daughter told me on the phone I had a problem, and the problem was that man. I wanted my family to leave me alone. I got so tired of going to counseling everyday. On Labor Day, I was laying in my bed. I started feeling sorry for myself. I got up and I looked in the mirror. I saw myself angry and going down. I had a very close friend. I would call her up and tell her about how he would abuse me. She gave me very good advice. I still wouldn't listen to her. I cried for several days. I wouldn't eat, I lost weight, and my hair came out. I stayed angry all the time. I didn't like myself. One day, I looked at the phone and I decided to call my sisters. My sister is a minister at a church. She has her own business. She was at her restaurant during the time I called. When I called her I began to cry on the phone. I told her that I needed her help because I couldn't help myself. I told her that I was in a bad abusive relationship and that I didn't know how to get out of it. I began to tell her how this man treated me and how he abuses me. She told all of her church members to stop what they were doing and please come around the phone. They prayed for me and I began to pray for myself also. When they where finished praying for me, I felt better. My sister encouraged me to leave him and don't take anything from him. She told me to get out of that relationship fast. I remembered her asking the Lord to tear the relationship apart. When I hung up the phone with my sister, I began to think about the lowdown things he did to me and how he would talk to me. I said to myself, "I am going to leave him." One day, I came home from work and he was sitting on my porch waiting for me. He had the nerve to ask me "What is wrong with you." I told him to go with me into the bedroom because I had something to tell him. We went in my bedroom. I sat on my bed and I had a lamp in my hand for protection. I told him to get out of my house right now before I really hurt him. I told him that I refused to let him continue to hurt me again. We had a bad argument. He began to come up close to me, but I told him if he didn't get back I would let him have it. He saw a strange look on my face and I told him to get out of my house. He wouldn't leave so I ran out the house to call the police. They wanted to put him in jail. I began to tell the police what David did to me. They were very upset at him. The police finally made him leave. He was very upset at me. I was so glad I left him. Each time I saw him, I went a different way. Whenever I see him I didn't even speak to him. I didn't converse with him at all. I stayed out of his way. My family asked me not to go around him at all. They told me that I shouldn't be anywhere he might be because he is angry with me. When I leave my house I could see him walking by my house. My family knows who he is and also the police know. My two daughters know where he is. My oldest daughter talked to him. She told him that she wants him to leave me alone. I felt good about myself. I am a new person. I don't go to counseling anymore. I get along with my oldest daughter now. I am in college. I am working toward my degree in counseling. I will be graduating in two more years. I am a very proud parent. I am an active church member. I am writing a book on women who have been abused. I want to be able to help other young women who are in abusive relationships. I want to help them to get out of it and know what to look for when you get in abusive relationships. I would like to tell every young lady don't let no man lower your character and take your respect from you. I would like to tell all women who is in abusive relationships that they are somebody. You are better than that and you don't have to stand low for a man. Now I have resided with my oldest daughter and she understands what this man took me through. The emotional, physical and mental abuse that he took me through makes me a stronger woman. I have no idea what God has in store for me. I was a young woman during the time when that happened. I thought this man loved me but I found out he didn't. It took a very long time for me to realize that he didn't love me. I felt like I needed someone to love and protect me, but he wasn't the right one for me. There is no way I would let another man take me through this punishment again. In the midst of me planning to get away from this person a big miracle happened in my life. I am in school trying to be a writer. I still have had time to think about how I was treated and abused. I am seeking out a support group. I am blessed to have such wonderful daughters. My oldest daughter has a very good job. She works for a major insurance company. She has 1-½ years of college left. She is planning to go back to school. My youngest daughter graduated from Tennessee State University. She has a degree in Social Science with a concentration in Psychology and History. I am very proud of myself. I still wake up in the middle of the night thinking about why this had to happen to me. I wake in the middle of the night screaming and trembling and crying in my sleep. I'm always thinking about the pain this man took me through. I still can't have a normal relationship because I treat men the way they treat me so I guess now I am the abuser. Not physically but perhaps emotionally. I can't trust, I can't go on always remembering and grieving. Always wondering what is going to happen to me. How will I treat a spouse or how do I treat the enemy. This is a beginning process, a healing process with the ability to be able to allow me to forgive myself. I need to get over being ashamed of myself. I need to be strong and say I can do this by the help of the Lord. I just need help. I need to find a way to think for myself everyday. Now I take it slow and relax when I come home from work and know that I can get over this. You don't need the abuse anymore. Most importantly know that you deserve better. Young ladies Don't wait until it's too late, and stay with an abusive person. Get out of it as soon as you see it happening. The biggest mistake you can make is to live with an abusive man. Make sure you tell yourself everyday, over and over until you believe in it. You are not addicted to the abuse; you are addicted to the man. This is not the kind of attention you need in your life. Ladies, love is out there, and you do deserve it. No matter how many times he says things like, "No one else will love you" or "no one can love you the way I do" or even "No one will want you," understand that there are good men that will love you for who you are. They will love the beautiful person inside of you. This man tried to control my life. I wouldn't let him control me. He would get angry with me and start cursing at me. Then he would try to fight me. I never experienced a man trying to fight me. He was the first man to ever abuse me. Sometimes I would see the abuse getting ready to start. Please don't wait too late before something bad happens to you. Get out of it! Tell a friend like I told my friends. Get help! You are not addicted to any man. That is your mind telling you that you can't get out of the abusive relationship. You can get out. You only have to make up your mind to do it, and you have to say to yourself like I did, "I am better than that. I am somebody." I deserved better. I also had to say that this was not me. I didn't know who that person was. Being born a Gemini, I can sometimes have two personalities—a good personality and a bad personality. My bad personality made me lose my self-esteem. Go to counseling, and get in a support group. Talk to yourself like I did. Think about what you are doing to yourself and your family. You are hurting your family. I know that my youngest daughter loves me. If I would have stayed in that abusive relationship, I know that I would either be in jail or dead because I would have really hurt him eventually. That would have really hurt her. I wouldn't want to do anything to hurt my daughters because I know that they need their mother, and they love me no matter what. I feel so good about myself now because I am abuse free. I'll never again put myself through another abusive relationship. I don't think a man is worth going through this again. I can laugh again. I can smile again. While I am very comfortable talking to men, I am not dating right now. I want to enjoy my life writing my book and counseling young ladies that have been in an abusive relationship. I would like to sit down and tell other young ladies how I was abused and treated by a man that didn't have anything to offer me. I don't want to see other young ladies make the same mistake that I made. There are women out there today thinking that they are in love and they want to be loved, but they are going the wrong way to finding love. Please listen to me and let me help you before it's too late. Please don't let any man bring you down. He is not worth it. Abuse is a mental illness. When a man abuses you, he is sick in the mind. When he was small, someone in his family abused him. When he grew up, he started abusing women. If he doesn't get some help, he could kill somebody. He turns into another person and that person inside might harm you. People who abuse others really don't know what they are doing. They are daydreaming. You have to stay away from those people. If you don't leave your problem, it is not going to get any better. He wants you to change. He wants to control you and have you afraid of him. People like that want you to feel sorry for them. You call that attention. He is looking for attention because he can't get it anywhere else. He thinks that he will come to you. You may feel like you are stupid and the cause of the abuse. Don't blame yourself for being in the abusive relationship because you didn't know he was that type of person. You thought you loved this person but you find out he didn't love you. I thank God I am out of that abusive relationship. I could have been dead. Who would have taken care of my daughters? My daughters and I are very close. I wouldn't want to hurt my family over a man. Domestic Violence really doesn't have to start in your home. It can start with anything that makes you feel unsafe in your own home or with being afraid of someone who wants to have control over you. It is really difficult when you find out that someone who you thought loves you really doesn't. Home is a place where a person should be able to feel safe. We think about older people experiencing violence because people try to take advantage of them, but anyone can be a victim of domestic violence. You can be married or even living together with some one you love. Women should be able to recognize situations that could become very dangerous to them and reach out to other women, who have been hurt. Men can be affected by violence as well and women too. It can happen to one of their loved ones. People need to understand the root of domestic violence against women and see how their own feelings and attitudes might make others think that domestic violence is okay. They also need to let other men know that it's wrong, and what you can do to end this bad problem. Go to counseling or get in an organization. They would really help you. You also can find place where you can get help or offer you help to end this terrible problem. You can also go to a support group. I had three years of violence with him. Things got worse, and then I decided to go for help. I began to ask myself why I would take this off this man. I asked myself several times saying, "Bell, what is wrong with you. You didn't take that off your husband." I was very surprised by my lack of action, and I was ashamed of myself. After long periods of abuse, women who have been involved in domestic violence begin to think that it is their fault. I didn't think it was my fault at all because this man has also been abused. When he was younger he was abused. He told me that his family abused him. Most men who grow up to be abusers are working out the abuse that they still have in them from their childhood. I had a lot of people try to tell me. I wouldn't listen. I know his uncle tried to tell me how he was. I wouldn't listen to him. I had to find this man out for myself. I am glad that I found out how this man is. I really don't think I would let another man treat me like this again. I really don't deserve this treatment. No woman deserves to be pushed, kicked, slapped, or knocked down to the floor. Women deserve to be loved and treated with respect. I made a mistake in my life. I would like to work together to make the world safe for women and try to stop this madness. Domestic violence is a mental disorder. I never thought I would ever make up my mind to get out of this bad relationship. It would only get worse. I knew that I had to leave this abusive relationship before it was too late. I feel good about myself knowing that I don't have anyone who wants to control me and try to destroy my life. I have to check a man out before I start dating him. It pays to ask people about him, but don't let him know you are asking about him. I talk with my friends about me being in a domestic violence relationship. They will say negative things like, "You have lost your mind." They would ask me, "What did your two daughters think of your being in an abusive relationship?" I know my friends and my daughters were very upset at me and very surprised of me. They couldn't understand me. They asked me, "Why mama? What is wrong with you? I thing you have lost your self-esteem." They prayed a lot for their mother. I know this wasn't me; it was another person inside of me that had the control over me. I wasn't happy in this relationship. I would go to church and sit crying throughout the whole service. I would go to work feeling bad and sad about my situation. I was ashamed of this man because I knew he was an alcoholic and abusive. I really didn't want to go out with him. When I would go out with him, I would walk in front of him because I didn't want anybody to know that he was with me. I told him that one day I was going to leave him, and it won't be too long. This man changed my whole life. I felt like I didn't have a life anymore. He wanted me all to himself. I couldn't speak to a man. He would accuse me of cheating on him. All this man wanted to do was control my life and keep me away from other men, who wanted to talk to me. When

I went somewhere, he would time me to make sure I went where I said I was going. He didn't trust me at all. I never had a man to say he didn't trust me. When I was married of the age of 22, in my young days, my own husband didn't treat me like that. My ex-husband never abused me. He just had a problem during that time. I left him at the age of 26. I am divorced and I haven't got married since. I am still trying to get over this bad abusive relationship that I was in. My pastor always advises young women and young men to give themselves time to heal between relationships rather than immediately jumping from one to the other. You are still hurting from the last relationship. I am not dating. I am a friend with several men. When they come up and ask to take me out to dinner, I go; however, I let them know that I am not looking to get in a relationship right now. I let them know that I have been hurt very badly and felt disrespected, and I don't want to go through that again. I am going to wait on the Lord for him to send me a nice Christian man. I have prayed and ask God to send me a saved man that enjoys going to church, like me. The next man I date will have to be a saved man because I refuse to date an unsaved man. It is important for a woman to set standards that are important to her for the person she wants to date so that she does not end up in a bad relationship.

I look over my life at times and I say to myself, "Bell what was wrong with you. Why did you let that man take you through this?" That was a bad experience for me. What woman wants to be in an abusive relationship? When I was in this relationship, things wouldn't go my way. I was very stressed out. I would find myself day dreaming of this relationship. My oldest daughter really did help me. She talked to this man, and told him to leave her mother alone. She meant that. Then she told me, "Mama I want you to stay away from this man." I did. This man did all he could do to try to get me back. He would go places where he knew I was going. He would show up at my job and stand outside waiting on me to see him. When I saw him, I would ignore him because I don't want him anymore. I am so glad that I didn't let him bring me down. I saw right through this man. I knew what he was trying to do to me. He was trying to use me and he wanted to have control. I found this man out. He is abusive. He enjoys abusing women and trying to get over on them.

This man is not the only person from whom I have suffered abuse. I have been abused on my job. I have worked for the school system for many years as a substitute teacher. My supervisor emotionally distresses me at work. They did all they could to try to make my day very hard for me. I was abused as a young girl of 12. When I was in school, I was abused. When I was 16 years old, I was raped by five men. Now you know how I feel about my life. I had a very hard life. I think about my life coming up and how I was treated during that time. I ask myself, "Why would a person do somebody like that?" I say to myself, "That is evil." I'm grown now, and I know all about what life is. I am a good woman, and it will have to be a good man for me to get involved. A bad man took everything out of me. He didn't appreciate me. A bad man treated me wrong and he used me. I am so glad that the Lord showed me how this man was. I am very proud of myself because I was able to let this man go. Now I feel better and I look better. I have moved on with my life. I'll never let another man treat me this way again. I am stronger and wiser now. It took me a very long time to find this man out. I didn't want anybody to tell me anything. I wanted to find out on my own. No woman should ever have to endure how I was treated. I didn't deserve this kind of treatment. I deserved better than that. No woman deserves to be slapped, knocked down and beat up like I was. That experience did something to me; it made me think about how women should be treated. I know that I got involved with the wrong type of men. I really cannot believe that I went that low for a man. Now I can help other young women that have been going through the same experience I went through. I don't want to see another woman go through what I went through because it is painful and fearful. This man and I were not compatible. Ladies try to find somebody that is on the same level as you. When you see that you are in an abusive relationship, get out of it before it starts. Tell a friend like I did. Talk to somebody before it is too late, if you don't he will take you out. Please don't stay in the relationship, get away from him because he is not going to change.

Being in a domestic violence relationship can happen in all kind of families and relationships. No one deserves to be abused. Women today deserve to be treated with love and kindness. The only person responsible for the abuse is the abuser. Please don't punish yourself and beat up yourself because you are not responsible for somebody else's mistakes. Abuse is an internal act that one person uses in a relationship to control the other. Abusers have learned to abuse so that they can get what they want. Abuse may be physical, sexual, emotional and psychological. The abuser usually has low self-esteem. They also do not take responsibility for their own actions. They may even blame the victim for causing the violence. In most cases, men abuse female victims. It is important to remember that women can also be abusers and men can be the victims. Abusers are not easy to spot. They may appear friendly and loving to their partners and family. They often only abuse behind closed doors. They also try to hide the abuse by causing injuries that could be hidden and do not need a doctor. There are some men who suffer from substance abuse such as drugs and alcohol. It is better to stay away from these types of people because they will hurt you and when they hurt you, they may not remember what they did to you. I was blessed because I immediately got out of my relationship. Watch the way the man treats you and his attitude. This will help you know when you are abused. Don't stay in the relationship because he is not going to change. That means he has a problem and it also means he may have been abused. I am so glad that I made up my mind and I got out. My abuse has not made me afraid to date again, but I feel like I will get hurt again. I am much more cautious of others. I have had many young men that wanted to date me. I tell them that I am not ready to date anybody yet. Just give me time to get over the relationship I was in. I think about how I was mistreated and taken advantage of. I ask myself how I could let this happen. I would like to know what I saw in this man. I really didn't see anything in him. This man wasn't my type of man. I saw right through this man. I saw the game this man was trying to play on me. My brother told me that he wasn't the type of man for me. I wouldn't listen to him or anyone, but I found him out for myself. I am so glad that the Lord showed me how this man was. I reaped what I sowed for dating that man. He tried to kill me. I thank God that I went on my way. It took me a very long time for me to wake up. When I see this man, I look at him and see what a fool I was. This man doesn't have anything going for himself. I don't need him. I said to myself, "My ex-husband didn't treat me like that. When I saw David, I would look the other way because I would get angry at myself and begin to think about how he slapped me and knocked me down in my own house. I got very upset at him because no one should have to feel that way. I give it to the Lord. I pray about it. I know God will take care of what he did to me. I know you don't do wrong and get by with it. I will forgive him. I ask God to forgive me for thinking that way. Maybe if it was another lady, that man might be dead, but I am not that type of woman. All I want to do is to move on with my life. I know that God has someone good for me. I cannot understand why a man would abuse women. I feel like when a man abuses a woman, he is jealous of her, and he has been abused in his life. I don't understand why a man would like to be in control of women. This man I was dating wanted to be in control of me and I didn't let him. He would fight me and he wanted me to be afraid of him. I knew he had a serious problem. Sometimes I think about all of the destructive things this man has done to me. I get very angry with myself and I ask myself why did I allow this man to do me like this. Sometimes I cry and I asked myself what was wrong with me because I couldn't understand what it was. I asked myself if I cared about this man. What was it about this man that drew me? What did you like so much about this man? I felt sorry for him. I thought I could help him. I thought I could reach out to him and help him. I saw how his family treated him and I just wanted to help. I found out that I couldn't help him. He didn't want to be helped. He liked the way he was, but he didn't realize that he was abusing himself. I am so happy that I am out of that abusive relationship. I got my life back again. I am happy, in church and I stay around Christian people. I smile more often. I am not under any stress. I thank God for taking me out of this relationship. When I see this man in the stores, I look at him and I shake my head and I say to myself what did I see in him? I go another way. He doesn't look the same anymore. I pray to the Lord that God will help him and turn his life around. Being in an abusive relationship is very scary. You don't know if you will make it out or not. It is just a give, give situation. When you make up your mind, you will get tired of going through all of those changes and getting abused. You will get out. I hope and pray that no woman would have to go through what I went through in an abusive relationship. That was very painful and frightening for me. I am very ashamed of myself, and I am very embarrassed. It is very embarrassing to my two daughters and my sister to let them know how stupid I was. I had to pray and ask God to help me to come back to myself. I had a lot of prayers that went up for me. I thank God for answering my prayers and I also thank the people that prayed for me. I hope that I can be some help to another young lady that is in an abusive relationship. I would like for that person to read my book and make sure that you understand what I went through before you start dating. Please check him out.

Abuse comes in all kind of ways such as screaming and yelling at each other, cursing, and name-calling. I can tell you more but those are some examples of abuse. If I can be any help to anybody. Please don't wait. I will sit you down and tell you my life story, about how I was abused and I will also counsel you. I am in college working on my degree in counseling so that I will be better qualified to help others in this and other tough situations. I really do hate this had to happen to me. I am ashamed of myself that this had to happen to me but angry because it did happen to me. This situation made me stronger and wiser and more cautious than I was before. Abuse is very hurtful mentally and physically. You feel like you can't be helped. Often times you don't understand why you are letting this happen to you. You ask yourself what you have done to deserve this kind of treatment. I still ask myself why I allowed this to happen to me. I am very stupid for allowing this to happen to me. I am very disappointed in myself because I let this happen to me over and over. I was led on to believe that this man cared about me. It took me a very long time to find him out. I never want to meet another man like him again. Now I stay to myself and I hope that I don't see this man again. I don't go around him. I really don't go any place where he may be. I just don't want to be around him. I will forgive him and I will let God take care of him. I will never forget what he did to me, and I will also never forget what my brother did to me when I was younger. I don't go around him. I told my two daughters what he did to me when I was a young girl. They didn't like what he did. They don't go around him either. I told both of them to stay away from him because he is sick. He is dangerous to be around also. My brother is a sex addict. He abuses young girls. Apparently, he didn't care what age they are. He would beat them up and take advantage of them. I am a witness to this. Everything he has done to those young girls, he did me the same way when I was young. The man I was dating abused me several times until I found out how he was. He almost tried to kill me. I am glad I am away from him because if I had stayed in that relationship, my oldest daughter probably would have hurt him. She warned him to stay away from me. She told him that she meant what she said. When she finally had a chance to talk to me, she cautioned me about him. She told me, "Mama, what do you see in him? He is an alcoholic, and he doesn't have anything going for him. He is an abuser, and you don't need him. He will end up killing you. I want you to leave that man alone. He is dangerous to be around, and he doesn't care about you. He is evil." My youngest daughter talked to me also. She asked me to leave him alone because she and her sister had both found him out. I am so glad that I listened to my daughters. I would probably be dead if I hadn't listened to them. My daughters love and care about me. They don't want to lose their mother over somebody that means her harm and not good. I want to accomplish things in my life such as trying to get my book together. I want to help other young women that have been abused in their relationships. I want to help young ladies and I don't want to see them make the same mistake that I made. I want to be able to tell them to move on with their lives and to leave before it's too late. I will tell every young lady that God didn't put women on this earth to be abused. He wants men to cherish us and love us. I made a mistake and I regret it. Now I am stronger and wiser.

I have moved on with my life. I don't want to look back at the past. Now I am looking toward the future. I am looking for better things in my life. When you have been abused, you feel bad and you are very depressed. You would like to talk it out with somebody. You don't know whom to trust because you don't want your business to be spread all over the world. I feel like when you have been abused by someone you should go to a counselor and talk about it. When I went to a counselor, I cried each time I talked about it. I can understand why this had to happen to me. The lady that I spoke with began to lift my spirits. She encouraged me to hold my head up and get out of that bad relationship because something bad could happen to me. I also met other victims who have been abused and often found ways to help with my problems. I was always depressed. I took depression pills and stayed upset all of the time. I couldn't eat, and it seemed that sleep did nothing for me. My daughters and I were always fussing and arguing. I use to get upset with her and distance myself from her. She use to always talk with me about this man, but I will get angry with her and yell at her. I use to always tell her she was wrong and disrespectful and I didn't want to hear what she had to say. I just wasn't a happy person. It even got so bad when I started to bring my problems to work. It made me less effective in dealing with the children. I couldn't concentrate at work and sometimes didn't want to go to work. When I had a conversation with someone I began to think that person was being abusive to me. I took the way people said things all wrong. I was hurting myself by allowing all of these things to affect my judgment. It was just something inside me that made me feel unworthy. But I know that wasn't' true. I was somebody and I didn't deserve that. No one deserves that kind of abuse. I often prayed and began to go to church more. Getting closer to God and having a relationship with God is what got me through. I was able to admit that I was abused. This is why I feel like I can help others by telling my story. I can advise people to get out of that relationship and take control of their life. We have all been abused in some way, whether by a family member or someone in a relationship. Sometimes people are ashamed to come forward to tell what is going on with them. They may not want anyone to know. But if you tell someone you can save a life.

Women who have been beaten by their husbands or boyfriends are called battered women. You may not understand "battered." Battered means beaten and women have been taken advantage of by these men. Many of these women allow their men to take advantage of them and control them. They don't want to lose their man. Women would lose their self-esteem and accept anything just to have somebody in their lives. When you meet a man, he may seem like he is so nice and so interested in you, but once you ignore the signs of domestic violence and allow this man to take control over everything, you have lost your respect because now he is going to change on you. Often times these women will isolate themselves from others because they are embarrassed and ashamed of what they have allowed. These men should be put away for life. Women need to know and understand that they are headed toward destruction. I don't want to live another day like this. I was headed to destruction myself, and then I realized that I was in danger and needed to get myself away. God looked down on me and he helped me get out of the horrible relationship alive. If it wasn't for the Lord, I would probably be lying in my grave now. Please don't let this happen to you. Please remember this is not the way life should be. I would like to counsel men that can't keep their Hands off of women. There are a lot of men walking around putting their hands on women. These men have a serious problem and need help. I remember talking to a man and asking him, "Why do men like to abuse women?" He said, "Maybe it builds their ego up and we like to think that we are in control. I also asked him, "Don't men know that it is wrong to abuse women?" He told me that they did know. I want to encourage men to read my book also. This may be a way to keep them from being violent towards their women. Personally, I don't want to be around a man that is abusive towards women. I have no respect for men like that. I would like to know how they feel when they beat women. I would like to know where their mind is. I think that they are sick in their mind and need some counseling help immediately. These men have some type of mental problem. I would like to run a study to determine the cause of domestic violence. A man really has to be out of his mind to beat up on women. Men like this are very dangerous and seriously ill but they will not go and get any professional help. I would like to go to the women's shelters and speak to the women and let them know that everything will be alright; it just depends on the person. I feel sorry for these ladies. Men have taken advantage of our young girls. They are using their bodies and abusing them. We need to stop violence against our women. When a woman has been abused and taken advantage of, she doesn't feel the same, and she is embarrassed. She often feels like something has been taken away from her. We, as women, want a man to respect us, cherish us, and love us. When a man has misused a woman and disrespected her, the woman feels like she is inadequate. That's the way I felt when I was abused. I cried and cried and ask myself why this had to happen to me. I wonder what I did to get this kind of treatment from a man. I said to myself I don't deserve this, and I am not going to let any man take my womanhood away from me. I am better than that. I said this man is trying to take everything from me. I lost every part of self-esteem I had. This situation took a lot out of me. I was weighted down with pain and hurt in fear. I didn't look like myself. My face broke out, and I lost my appearance. I wasn't a happy woman. I tried to make myself happy but I couldn't. All I could think about how I was abused and I wanted to get out of it. I kept some things to myself. I got tried of this and decided to tell somebody I was close to. That was my two sisters, who are ministers. They told me that they demanded that I get out of this relationship before this man really hurt me. They wanted to know what was wrong with me that I would allow myself to get involved with this man. They began to pray for me, and they had the members of their church to pray for me also. God broke that control spirit away. I just want women to keep themselves from going through what I went through. I lived in fear with this man. Now he is paying for what he did to me. He is a really sick man. I will forgive him and ask God to save him. I hold no grudges against anyone in my heart. I've got to forgive him because God forgives us for our sins. I can't walk around this earth not forgiving anyone. I have never had a man to treat me like this before. Words cannot explain how I feel deep down inside. I say I have been through a lot, but I will never let another man take me through this again. I think about it and I try to keep myself busy by reading, looking on the internet of things concerning my next book. Sometimes when I get off from work, I go to the library and check out two or three books. I bring the books home with me and I sit up half of the night and read. I began writing down whatever comes to my mind. God speaks to me and he guides me through writing my books. I m writing another book called, "Let him go before he destroys you." He will destroy you. Domestic

Violence is a serious crime; you don't know how you will come out of it. You might be dead if you stay. Why would you want to date a man that will damage you and your life? Didn't he show you the signs that he had mental problems? I don't care what anyone says. Women don't deserve to be beaten and abused by a man. I am not going to take up for a man when he is wrong. He needs to be punished for the crimes he commits. I don't know what makes these men feel like this. God is going to put a stop to this crime. I am going to keep on praying for the men who are abusing their women. This crime has been going on for a long time. Don't you see we are losing our young women because of domestic violence? I watch the news Every day, women are beaten and raped. Lately, elderly women have been beaten and raped. How could anyone beat and rape an elderly woman and walk around like nothing has happened? This woman is somebody's mother, grandmother, sister, or aunt that they are taking advantage of. How would they feel if somebody did their mother like this? I know you can't do wrong and get by with it. Sooner or later you will be caught. My attentions are to help women get out of domestic violence relationships and encourage them to leave this man before he kills them. God will send you a good man one day. I enjoy my life the way I am. I have been out of this abusive relationship going on four years now. I work for a county school system. I go to church a lot. I go to Wednesday night Bible study and services on Sunday morning. Sometimes I go back to church on Sunday evenings. I put my time in church and I do my homework. I attend Grand Canyon University. I am working on my degree in Psychology. I will be graduating in 2010 or 2011. After graduation, I plan to go back for my master's degree in professional counseling. I want to counsel young women that have been abused. I am looking forward to getting my own business in the future. I enjoy writing books. I like to write all day long. Reading relaxes my mind, and writing opens my knowledge. I work out a lot. I go to the gym three times a week. I stay mostly to myself, rather than running around with a lot of other women. I want to go out and speak on behalf of my book. I want to speak at different colleges and churches all over the world. Wherever God leads me, I want to give some knowledge to these women. I also want to go on national television and speak to people over the world. I am looking forward to being in the spotlight not for fame but to help those out who struggle with domestic violence. My heart goes out to these women who have been abused. I know exactly what they are going through; I went through the same experience. I want to be a blessing to someone; I want to reach out to people. I want to show love and kindness to these women and show them that I care. You never know how much help this book could offer. I am praying this book will help people. People just want a normal life and domestic violence is not normal. I later asked David why he did this to me. He told me that he didn't know. I just looked at him and told him that something was seriously wrong with him. I also told him that he was sick, and that I couldn't believe that he was telling me that he didn't know why he beat women like they are animals. I said this man has to be bipolar. I will never get myself involved with another person like him. I didn't know he had all those problems. I am so happy that I found this man out before he destroyed me. I know I was headed toward destruction. I got another chance. Don't let a man bring you down. Remember we are to be loved and cherish. I have realized that all men are not the same. I am afraid to take myself through this type of relationship again. Men try to talk to me all the time but I just tell them that I am not ready to date right now. I don't want to seem like I am downing all men because there are some good men out there.

In society today, domestic violence against women has raised eyebrows. Approximately 1.8 million women are battered each year. Many people in our country believe that domestic violence against women is the major cause of injury to women, exceeding muggings, rapes, and auto accidents combined. Therefore, the U.S. Department of Justice discovered that 95% of assaults on spouses or ex-spouses are committed by men against women. However, only 20% of female trauma cases are victims of injury by an acquaintance or husband. Every nine seconds, a woman is abused by her husband or intimate partner. Domestic violence affects individuals, families, and society in general. Injuries received by victims of domestic violence are at least as serious as those suffered in 90% of violent felonies. So what is domestic violence?

Domestic violence not only includes physical abuse. It also includes sexual and psychological abuse and destruction of property. Physical abuse includes all types of aggressive behavior such as choking, using an object to hit, twisting of body parts, use of weapons, punching, etc. Sexual abuse includes attack on the victim's breast or genital area, unwanted sexual behavior or intimacy forced on someone. Psychological abuse often reflects threats of being killed, isolation, and frequently occurring physical attacks. Forcing the victim into doing degrading things such as eating animals and performing other sex acts are also forms of psychological abuse. Destruction of property usually takes place without physical attack; however, it is still considered a type of abuse. It has been determined that 90% of all married couples who are seeking counseling have engaged in some type of physical abuse. Domestic violence is sometimes referred to as battering. Battering is always associated with control over an intimate partner or family member.

Domestic violence is a widespread problem among all socioeconomic levels. In most American families it has been found that between 53% and 70% of male batterers also abuse their children. In 1992, studies indicate that there were 128,000 cases of child physical and sexual abuse. It has also been discovered that 1 in 5 female children are often times sexual molested.

Violence growth has increased so much in today's society; Traumatic stress can sometimes have an effect on the events of domestic violence in the family. The

Diagnostic and Statistical Manual of Mental Disorder suggests that repeated exposure to traumatic events can cause an individual to develop some type of mental disorder, such as posttraumatic stress disorder. Traumatic stress refers to the feelings, thoughts, actions and physical reactions of individuals who are exposed to, or who witness, events. In some domestic violence situations, children may get an excessive amount of exposure to violence in their preschool and kindergarten years. Most of the time more than half of the school-age children experience posttraumatic stress disorder due to domestic violence. If these children are not treated, the children may become delinquents, substance abusers, school drop outs and may experience difficulties in their own relationships. We have to realize children express themselves better verbally. Young children may become withdrawn, non-verbal, experience difficulties sleeping, and anxiety issues. However, girls are more likely to become withdrawn. 30 to 50 % of these adolescents are at risk of academic failure. They drop out of school and abuse drugs because of their exposure to violence. Batterers have different characteristics. One characteristic is that most batterers are in need of love. Most of the time the batterer wants to feel like they are loved by somebody or they want to be shown some love. Another characteristic is they use violence to get their way with their partner. The batterer wants to feel like he or she is in control. Often times they are stubborn because they always want to have their cake and eat it too. They tend to be critical or jealous of their partners. In my opinion, jealousy can be one of the causes of domestic violence. He or she may not want their partner to leave the house, dress sexy or communicate with other people, mainly due to jealousy. Also they don't take on responsibly for their behaviors and often times deny that abuse happens. The batterer may say "It was not me" or they may say "You made me do it." They will not take on the consequence of their behaviors. They also may refer to the abuse as just talking. They will completely deny the fact that it's considered abuse. Their main purpose goal in abuse is CONTROL. Abuse is about control and selfish power over someone. It's almost similar to bullies in a schoolyard. Abusers are usually described as coming from all races, religions, and income levels. Often they come from abusive family backgrounds. Abuse in the privacy of the home often goes unknown. The abuser shows remorse after the abuse keeping the family from reporting it. Abusers often suffer from low self-esteem, are impulsive, and become easily frustrated. The victims may or may not come from an abusive background. Often they believe they are the cause of the abuse. They may not recognize the person as an abuser because he appeared to be calm and controlled while dating. The victim may also be afraid to inform anyone of the abuse. The victim sometimes stays in domestic violence relationships because they believe they are not stable economically and socially. According to the author of *It's not okay anymore,* "Some victims, even women who are successful in other parts of their lives, come to believe that abuse is their destiny and the best they can hope for." Abuse is not a destiny. Like survivors around the world, you can change your situation now. Your destiny is in your hands, not your partner's. In many cases abuse has the same impact as brainwashing a person. There is usually an increase in isolation from people and resources such as money and the family car. There are several behaviors which are used to control the victim's fear. Humiliation destroys the person's self-esteem especially if abuse occurs around others. Control is taken over, making all of the decisions and activities. Trivial demands paralyze the victim's energy to be resistant. The victim hopes that things will change. She is reminded that the abuser is capable of doing her right. She indulges this hope rather than seeking help. Demonstrations of power teach the victim that she is helpless in the relationship. Dependence develops as the victim loses control over her activities, choices, thoughts and opinions.

In domestic violence there is a cycle of violence that occurs before, during and after the situation. There are three distinct phases of violence. First is tension building. Some abusive incidents occurs and tension is building up. Often times the victim tries to make the situation better by apologizing, accepting the blame, making promises to better the situation. For example, the victim may defend the abuser. "He didn't mean to do it." "He couldn't help himself. Next time, I have to try harder to show him that I love him and do what he wants." Step two, the tension escalates and violence eventually occurs. Step three is apology and forgiveness. The abuser sometimes expresses how sorry and confused he is by the behavior. They may do things to make up for the abuse such as make promises that it'll never happen again and buy gifts. For example from the story of Ike and Tina Turner in the movie, *What's Love Got To Do With It?* The first time Ike beat Tina, he went out and bought her a beautiful dress as an apology to make up for the abuse. It's the honeymoon cycle. Everything seems great because both the victim and abuser apologizes and makes promises. The victim may cook his favor meal or buy new lingerie. Then the relationship returns to its regular routine with its normal ups and downs. Now tension is building up again. Different things are starting to upset him. The victim pulls the trigger—something that sets him off. It could be that the victim is late coming home, hasn't completed laundry, or just doesn't have enough food in the house. Abuse happens again. Abusive men, because of their low self-esteem and insecurity, take every event that happens as an attack toward them. They react with violent behavior. Since many of them have been physically, emotionally, and sexually abused as children, they do not have the ability to trust others in their lives. The abuser sometimes has difficulties with other relationships and becomes critical or jealous of their spouse. They are also hungry for control. The batterer may have related drug or alcohol problems. They may also have a fear of intimacy. Often times the abuser may have strong feelings of guilt and failure, also denial of responsibility for their behavior, especially the violence.

There are three theoretical explanations for the character of an abusive man. They are psychoanalytical, social learner, and sociopolitical theories.

According to Gondolf, the psychologists' theories focus mainly on stress, anxiety, and anger during the man's childhood. The social learning theory focuses on the growth of aggressive communication on the part of both the husband and the wife. The sociopolitical theories refer to the power played by men. In early studies, researchers have discovered that women brought the battering on themselves. However, more recent studies suggest that battered women tolerate or seek abuse. Therefore, the men who battered are characterized as fearful and hateful toward women because of their childhood. There is always an issue of control. Men who batter are sometimes viewed as individuals who control their wives as a sense of self-esteem, authority, and privilege. One way a husband may control his wife is by withholding possessions, money, or access to the family car to isolate and intimidate her.

There are several signs of domestic violence. One would be frequent injuries that are excused as accidents.

Other signs are harassing phone calls from the partner and personality changes. An outgoing woman may become very withdrawn and absent. She may isolate herself from family and friends. Depression, crying, and low self-esteem can also indicate abuse.

Researchers have also discovered that 25% of all victims of domestic violence are pregnant women. Pregnancy is a risk factor for abuse. When abuse is present during pregnancy it can cause miscarriage, premature births, birth defects and learning disabilities. Also one in seven women are raped by her husband sometime during their relationship. One in four has an unwanted sexual experience. Other studies have also revealed that 34% of battered women had been raped in their marriage at least once. Domestic violence is present in every social, economic, racial, educational and religious group in society. A woman's cultural and religious beliefs along with her family background may influence her perception of abuse, but none of those things exempt her from the possibility of abuse. Two thousand children die each year from being abused by a parent or guardian. Forty-two percent of murdered women are killed by their intimate male partners. It is estimated that one in two women will be abused during their marriage. A national survey found that one out of six couples experience at least one violent act, and one in eight have an abusive act that causes injury to a partner.

There are several myths and misunderstandings about battering and domestic violence. Many people believe that religious beliefs will prevent battering. However, religious men are equally involved in battering. Also, people believe that women who are battered are uneducated and have few job skills, but the women who are battered are usually more educated and at greater risk of being abused by a partner. One major myth is that drinking is the cause of most battering behavior. Alcoholic drinks may reinforce the abuse but are not a major cause of abuse. Many believe that once someone is a batterer, he is always a batterer. However, men can eventually change with courage and help from others. Some people believe that sometimes battered women are getting what they deserve, but there is no justification for male violence. It is a criminal act of violence. The act of violence is likely to emotionally impair the children; therefore, children do not need their violent father around. Sometimes women stay for the sake of the children. This will only harm the well being of the children.

Everyone wants to know why women stay in domestic violence relationships. Many women feel like they have control over the situation. They feel as if there is hope for the relationship. They remain at risk in these domestic violence relationships because they believe they need the help and resources of the person who is abusing them. They also believe that the violence will eventually stop at some point.

Today, every state has some type of legislation designed to protect the victims of domestic violence. A lot of states require the police to make arrests, bring the victim to safety, and inform them of their legal rights. One of the most important laws associated with domestic violence is protective orders or restraining orders, which is a court order that directs the batterer to stop abusing the victim. In some states, the protective order may require the batterer to leave the shared residence and seek counseling. If the batterer violates the protective order, the batterer could be arrested. There could also be criminal action taken against the batterer including prosecution for assault, battery, aggravated assault, harassment and attempted murder. During the mid 1970's, an assault against wives or women was considered a misdemeanor in most states. Assault against a stranger was considered a felony. The current federal policy and law in some states is that domestic violence is a crime. Safety for victims of domestic violence and their children must be a priority. Changes in services, including medical care, are needed to help abused women.

Living in an abusive relationship takes a tremendous toll on a woman's physical and psychological well-being. If a woman is in an abusive relationship she should seek help from a physician. The physician should respond to the JCAHO, the Joint Commission on Accreditation of Healthcare Organizations, which requires that all hospitals enforce policies and procedures for identifying, treating and referring victims of abuse. It also requires educational programs for victims of domestic violence. Physicians can help battered women regain control of their lives. The AMA team is working extremely hard in an effort to reduce violence among women. Domestic violence has been viewed as a family matter which does not need the help of the government or criminal justice system. Often, spousal abuse is brought to the attention of hospitals and family physicians.

By seeking help from law enforcement officers, they are using the criminal justice system to accommodate and protect the victim. Usually when the police is involved in a domestic violence situation, they are there to keep the situation under control and see that the abuser leaves the residence if shared. Nowadays, police officers are trained to arrest the abuser instead of trying to keep the peace. They are to protect the victim and refer the victim to shelters and other community support groups that are available to help women who are being abused.

The Family Justice Initiative is a system established by President Bush that works toward eliminating domestic violence in our Nation. It provides assistance and service for victims of domestic violence allowing professionals, advocates, law enforcement, and organizations to come together. In 2006, the President signed legislation that reauthorized law enforcement to seek legal action against violence, sexual assault, and stalking. The Department of Justice Domestic Violence Transitional Housing Assistance Program provides assistance and housing services while working to move victims of violence into permanent housing.

According to the Office of Women's Health in the Department of Health and Human Services: "All women, children and men have the right to live their lives in a healthy and safe environment and to conduct their lives without emotional physical or sexual abuse or the fear of abuse. The mission of this agency is to work toward eliminating domestic violence and sexual assault and to reduce their effects in our community through crisis intervention, service education and community involvement" (Domestic Violence and Sexual Assault Coalition).

There are steps and different ways to get out of domestic violence situations. The National Domestic Violence Hotline provides crisis intervention and referrals to state resources such as shelters and help centers. Hospital emergency rooms treat injuries, and safe housing is provided. Women's shelters and crisis centers provide 24-hour emergency shelters for victims and their children. They also provide monitoring of the abuser. Mental health centers are also there to help victims. They provide individual counseling and support groups to women in abusive relationships. The local court can help the victim seek a court order which legally demands the abuser to stay away from the victim or they will face arrest. These programs are designed to accommodate the victim, to provide protection, and a new beginning in their lives.

In conclusion, everyone has the right to a violence free, safe and healthy life. Domestic violence is a criminal act. Therefore, it should not be treated as a family problem. I found it extremely important to report any crime of domestic violence. Abuse, in my opinion, is considered a health problem because it brings about different types of health issues to the victims such as posttraumatic stress disorder and injuries to the body. Every nine seconds a women is being battered by a partner. Within the last year, approximately 3.9 million women in America who are married or in a relationship were abused. That is 7% of American women in a year. There has to be something done about the issue of domestic violence. In my opinion, today society puts up with domestic violence as a family issue. Often times when the law enforcement is called in response to a domestic violence situation, it is usually brushed away. A person has to be seriously injured before they want to act like real law enforcers. The justice system has to be more in tune with domestic violence against women. Because domestic violence against women is sometimes ignored, the abuser has to be trespassing or destroying property for the police to take legal actions. Domestic violence is prominent in all socioeconomic groups and ethnic backgrounds. No one race or class levels are associated with domestic violence. There are many perspectives and preventions to domestic violence. In the United States, domestic violence against women is the single major injury to women, out weighting muggings, rapes, and auto accidents combined. Approximately, $3-5 billion dollars is spent yearly to treat victims of domestic violence. Different trends and perspectives will improve awareness of domestic violence and work towards reducing violence among women.

There are steps and different ways to get out of domestic violence relationships. The national domestic violence hotline has been offered to you. It provides crisis intervention plans and referral to state resources such as shelters, help centers, hospital emergency rooms, and safe housing sites. Women's homeless shelters or crisis centers provide a 24-hour emergency shelter for the victims and children. They also provide monitoring of the abuser. Mental health centers are also there to help victims. They provides individual counseling and support groups. These programs are designed to accommodate you in any domestic violence situation. It has been found that 90% of all married couples that are seeking counseling have engaged in some type of physical abuse during their marriage. Domestic violence is sometimes referred to as battering. Domestic violence is a widespread problem, which is among all socioeconomic level. In most American families it has been found that between 5% and 70% of male batterers also abuse their children in 1992. Studies shows that there were 128,000 cases of child physical and sexual abuse. It has also been found that 1 in 5 female children are often times sexually molested. There has been a rapid growth of violence in today's society. The diagnostics and statistical manual of mental disorders suggest that repeated exposure to traumatic events could cause an individual to develop some type of mental disorder such as posttraumatic stress disorder. Posttraumatic stress Disorder refers to the feelings, thoughts, actions, and physical reactions of an individual who is exposed to or witnesses events in a domestic violence case. Children receive a tremendous amount of exposure to violence in their pre-school and kindergarten years. More than half of the school-age children experience posttraumatic stress disorder due to domestic violence. If the child is not treated, the child may become a juvenile delinquent, substance abuser, school drop out and may experience the same violence in their relationships as they grow up. We have to realize children express themselves better verbally. Young children may become withdrawn, non-verbal, sleeping more often and have anxiety issues. However, girls are more likely to become withdrawn. Adolescents are at risk of academic failure because of the exposure to violence. They may drop out of school as a way to act out their problems. Adolescents are more attached to their parents and may experience verbal and physical abuse in relationships with parents during their adolescent years. Like many other survivors you can change your situation around. Your destiny is in your hands, not your partner's. Your life will change when you change. In many cases abuse has the same impact and brain washing a person. Researchers have also discovered that 25% of all victims of domestic violence are pregnant women. Pregnancy is a risk factor for abuse. When abuse is present during pregnancy it can cause a miscarriage, premature birth, birth defects and learning disabilities. Also, one in seven women have an unwanted sexual experience. Other students have also revealed that 34% of battered women had been raped in their marriage at least once. It is estimated that one in two women will be abused during their marriage. Don't wait until it's too late and stay with an abusive person. You can live without the abuse. Make sure that you tell yourself that. Repeat it over and over until you believe it. You are not addicted to the man. You are addicted to the abuse. It's not the kind of attention you need in your life. There is love out there and you deserve it. An abuser will use a lot of lines on you to keep you. He'll say things like, "No one else will love you. No one can love you the way that I do, or No one will want you because you are so stupid. No matter how many times he uses these and other lines on you, you must care enough about yourself to get out of the relationship. There are men out there that will love you for the beautiful person you are inside, and they don't care what baggage you bring. They just want to care for you and love you. I have shared only a crumb of my life, but I hope it helps you if you are out there in a bad situation. Remember you are not alone. There are people like me out here that care about you. After all, we are family bonded by the emotional ghost of our past. Find a shelter and make a plan. Then leave and never look back. Get help by talking to someone. Don't be ashamed of the pain or hide the truth. Let it out and talk to someone. The sooner you realize that none of this is your fault and that help is available in the form of caring people, the sooner you get to live free. You'll be able to look at yourself in the mirror again. Start believing in yourself. I hope my life and my story has helped someone. I believe in you; Now believe in yourself. As I sit and read so many articles on domestic violence and I think about me and how I was treated tears roll down my face. There are so many memories and so much pain in my life. Some physical and mental abuse was still there. I had grown all my life with abuse and did not know how that had taught me to be involved in constant abuse in my life. I have had nightmares all of my life and I still have nightmares to this day. Now, I can many times lie down to get a decent night rest. I was abused and I was living on my own instead of feeling good about myself. I felt like I needed protection from a man. I really needed someone to counsel me because my idea of love was all wrong. I found out when I was dating this man. I became so tired of being abused and tired of the beating. I have two daughters, and I am very blessed to have them. They love their mother. I am very blessed to have such wonderful beautiful young ladies. I have kept them away from all the abusive situations. They both saw what I went through. I couldn't take any of it anymore. The pain from the circumstances of the past was enough pain for a lifetime. I have been abused for three years. I still cannot sleep sometimes. I still wake up and someone will be there watching me. I wake up in the middle of the night crying and screaming in my sleep. Some nights I do not sleep. I do not recommend anyone being in an abusive relationship. It is the most undesirable, disrespectful and most terrible thing I have ever been in. I lost my best friend because of an abusive relationship; her boyfriend murdered her. I think about her a lot. This man was very cruel to her and abusive. Being in an abusive relationship you are surrounded by loss of self-esteem, depression, and so many other things. I still cannot have a normal relationship because I treat men now the way I have been treated. I am the abuser, not physically but emotionally. I cannot trust, and I cannot go out without always remembering what happened to me. Now, I have to ask myself how do I treat my spouse. Am I treating him like the enemy? It is a learning process, a healing process with the ability to be able to forgive yourself and others. Forgiving yourself is the first step and realizing that none of this is my fault. Get over being ashamed of yourself. Be strong and get away. Always say I can do this on my own. I just need help. Find a way to think for yourself everyday. Start off slowly when you have those five minutes in the shower to think. The next step is to know it is time to leave, and think of a way to do it. Pick a date, and plan it out. Be strong and know that you can do this no matter how badly you've been treated. Domestic violence affects more than 32 million Americans, ten percent of the U.S. population. Popular emphasis has tended to be on women as the victims. However, with the rise of the men's movement and men's rights, there is now an advocacy for men victimized by women. Women undergoing emotional abuse often suffer from depression, which puts them at increased risk for suicide, eating disorders, and substance abuse. Domestic violence against women in lesbian relationships is about as common as domestic violence against women in heterosexual relationships. In some relationships, violence arises out of a perceived need for power and control. It is a form of bullying and social learning of the abuser. Efforts to dominate their partners has been attributed to low self-esteem or feelings of unresolved childhood conflicts. Other factors are the stress of poverty and resentment toward women. There may be hostility and resentment toward men also. Personality disorders, genetic tendencies, and sociocultural influences are among other possible factors. Most authorities seem to agree that abusive personalities result from a combination of factors. One view of domestic violence is that it is a strategy to gain and maintain power and control over the victim but even in achieving this, it cannot resolve the powerlessness driving it. Such behaviors are addictive leading to a cycle of abuse or violence. Mutual cycles of abuse occur when each party is attempting to resolve his/her own powerlessness by exerting control. Other factors associated with domestic violence include heavy alcohol consumption and mental illness. Research has shown that alcohol-related violence is related to high levels of fluid. Response to domestic violence is typically a combined effort between law enforcement agencies, the court, and service agencies. Domestic violence has been moved more into the public view rather than just as a private family matter. Police officers try to ask one of the partners to leave the residence for a period of time. Domestic violence was considered as a misdemeanor offense. Abuse does not happen because someone is stressed out or using drugs. Abuse is an intentional act that one person uses in relationships to control the other. The abuser has learned to abuse so that they can get what they want. The abuse may be physical, sexual, or emotional. Abusers often have low self-esteem. They do not take responsibility for their actions. They may even blame the victim for causing the violence. It is important to remember the women can also be the abuser and men can be the victims. Abuse can start when the abuser gets angry. Sometimes there is poor communication. Often times the tension can become overwhelming and too much to handle. When the abuser feels guilty of what they did to their spouse, they usually make up by buying gifts. Being in an abusive relationship the abuser may tell you that it will never happen again. Please don't fall for that because I thought the man I was dating wasn't going to abuse me again, but he did it again. They will say anything just to get back with you. Never trust abusers. If he did it once, he may do it again. Abusers have a lot of anger inside of them. They usually take all their frustrations out on you. You never know when they will strike again. You have to be aware of those kinds of people because they are very dangerous. The abuser will act like the situation never happened. In your mind you know that this happened to you. When I was abused, this man called me the same day. My daughter answered the phone. She asked him where the bruises on her mother's arms and back came from. He lied to her and replied that it was just a misunderstanding. When somebody abuse you they are in denial and just don't want to admit they are wrong, mainly because they are ashamed of what they did to you. Most of the time, they don't want anybody to know they are abusing you. I have been physically and mentally abused in all kinds of ways, such as teenagers destroying my house by egging on Halloween. My house has been damaged three different times. I have had children to spray paint terrible words on my house. On my job, I have mean coworkers and I have been talked to in the most disrespectful way possible. I just let the Lord take care of them, and I know He will. That will not stop me from trying to help those who are going through the same situations of abuse as me. If you feel like your life is in danger, you can call the domestic violence hotline and call 911 because they can protect you. They will arrest your abuser if you have enough proof that you have been abused. When the police come, show the marks on your body that he put on you, and the police will have their proof of domestic violence. You can also take pictures of your bruises, which will also be considered as proof of domestic violence. This can be used when you go to court. Make sure you take that picture with you also. That will be your proof. If you don't have any place to go you can also tell the police, and they will provide you with information as to domestic violence programs and shelters for women and their children. Make sure the officer completes a police report, which could be used as evidence in court. I suggest you tell your family or friends and co-workers what has been happening to you. Tell them that you have been in a domestic violence relationship, and explain how long you have been in the relationship. I really don't think it is fair for the woman to leave her home because of what her abuser has done to her. End the relationship completely with him. There are a lot of women who had a chance to get out of the relationship, but they waited until it was too late. Once a woman allows her abuser to come back to her, he may do it again because abuse is an intentional act. The abuser likes control because he thinks you are weak. It is hard to stay away from these types of people; however, you have to be strong, put your foot down and say this is enough. My abuser really tried to beat me down, but I would not allow him to do that. I won't allow anybody to take away the things I've worked so hard for and accomplished. I've worked very hard to get where I am at now. I am worth more than that. Any of you who are in an abusive relationship can be comforted that the Lord brought me out. That lets you know that He can bring you out also. I will tell any woman to let the abusive man go and don't look back at him. Go forward with your life and find a good man. I promised myself that I would never put myself through this again. I almost lost my life as a result of domestic violence. I can always get another man but I can never get another life. Men should love women and cherish them rather than abuse them. You should take my advice and follow my story. I hate to see any woman go through abuse like I did. You may not make it out like I did. Women, we are going to stand up to these men and tell them we are not going to take their abuse any more. I refuse to take this kind of treatment anymore. I am going on with my life. I am waiting on a good man. I got off to myself and I prayed about my situation. I made up my mind what I was going to do. I had to do this on my own. I know if I had stayed in this relationship, my oldest daughter probably would have really hurt this man. I love my daughter; I didn't want to see her go to jail because of me. All you've got to do is think about all of the bad things this man did to you and about all of the physical, mental, and emotional abuse. I still get very upset at myself and wonder why I allowed this man to do this to me. I broke down and cried every night. I couldn't say anything because I allowed him to do me like this. My two daughters were very surprised of me. They said, "Mama, you are a very attractive young woman with class and knowledge. I don't understand why you would let someone do this to you. Any man would be glad to date you because you are smart and classy." I broke down into tears. I thought about everything I went through. I decided that I am going to move on with my life, and that is what I did. I felt good about myself. I knew I could do it. If I did it, you can to. Please don't wait too late. If you need some type of guidance and understanding you can email me at ratliffwillie@yahoo.com. I will be glad to make it my duty to talk with you and counsel you on this situation.

Please get out of this domestic violence relationship before your abuser takes you out. He is not worth it. You don't want to hurt your family and friends over a man who meant you nothing but evil. I had to learn this for myself. I had to go through this horrible relationship before I woke up. I don't want to see another women go through what I did. It really hurts when you thought someone loved and cared for you, and you find out that he just wanted to control and abuse you. He is your enemy. If I had known how this man was, I would have never gotten involved with him. I wish I would have listened to my friends. An elder lady told me about this man, but I wouldn't listen. I had to go through all of this abuse to find out what type of person he was. I just wouldn't listen to people. I wanted to find him out for myself. Maybe it took that for me to find him out. I know I will never let this happen to me again; I mean that. This was a bad experience for me. When young ladies have been abused by their mate, it brings to mind my best friend who was beaten up terribly by her mate. She eventually died from the abuse. Abusers are very dangerous and they have a lot of issues in their life. You never know when they will go off and strike you again. You have to be very careful when you around an abuser.

Some women may ask how to recognize an abusive man. There are plenty of signs that point to an abusive person. Watch how he treats you and how he talks to you. When you notice a man being overly aggressive and demanding, he may be an abusive person. You should just let him go. Don't get yourself tied up in an abusive relationship. He will play you and use you. If you are scared and want to talk to someone, talk with friends and family members. Please don't wait until it's too late to talk to someone. You can protect yourself. I told my daughters, my best friends and my family members. I wasn't scared to tell someone I wanted my family to know because we are very close. My daughters always try to keep up with me. They always want to know where I am all the time. They get worried if they don't hear from me everyday. I am blessed to have two daughters that care for me. Now since I am not in that relationship anymore, I feel safe and happy because I am out of it. I will never send myself through this again. I am so sorry I let this happen to me. You learn from your mistakes. I wish I had listened to other people. Sometimes you would say this is your fault for not listening. I can't beat myself up about it. I just have to let that be a learning experience for me. When women have been abused, that man has made it hard for the next man to establish a good relationship with the victim because the woman will be afraid to date. She may feel like that man will treat her the same way. Some women I talk to tell me that all men are alike. I tell them, "NO, you just haven't found the right one yet." I don't feel like that because there are some good men and there are bad men. A real man wouldn't put his hands on a woman and abuse her. David tried to make me lose my respect for myself. I lost my self-esteem and went into depression. I stayed off to myself. I felt sorry for myself. I felt like nobody cared about me. Often times, I found myself daydreaming about my problem. I cried at night. When people called me on the phone, they asked me why I sounded so sad and what was wrong with me. I wouldn't tell them what was really wrong with me. I would hang up the phone and cry myself to sleep. The next morning when it was time to get up and go to work, I didn't feel like going at all. I would take my anger out on other people. I would stay upset all the time. No one could say anything to me or I would go off on him or her. I really didn't want to be bothered with anybody. I was alone. I knew something was wrong with me. I wasn't a happy woman. I decided to go to counseling. I talked to the counselor and I told them what was happening to me. I knew I needed some help, and I wanted to get out of this bad abusive relationship fast. I went to counseling about a year. This nice counselor helped me. I never forgot what she told me. She asked me, "Mrs. Ratliff, what are you going to do?" I cried in front of this woman. I told her that I was going to get out of it. Every month I went to counseling. I began to get stronger listening to her. I took heed to what she told me. She told me to hurry up and get out of it before he destroys my life. I did what she asked me to do. I stayed away from him for a long time. I wouldn't talk to him on the phone. I wouldn't go to places where he would be so he couldn't see me. I finally got away from him by the help of the Lord. Sometimes I think about how he treated me. I get upset at myself. I try not to think about that so much because that is my past, and this man was my enemy. I never would've thought this man would be my enemy. He really surprised me. When I found out that I had an enemy, I would rather not be around him because I know what enemies will do to you. I know you have to help yourself if you make up your mind to get out of this abusive relationship. No woman wants to be with anybody who is abusive to them. I didn't know how to get out of it. There is help out there if you want it.

Men know how you feel about them and they will try to buy their way back into your life. Abusers like to be in control of you. They also want you to be afraid of them. Once you show them that they got you, they will do whatever they want to do. That is the way a man will take advantage of a woman and try to use her because she is afraid of him. If you don't get out of it, this man will take you out. Please don't wait until it's too late. Think about what Mrs. Ratliff went through in her relationship. I was blessed to make it out. If I had understood how this man was when I met him, I wouldn't have wasted my time on an abusive man like him. I got myself in a bad situation, and I regret every minute of it. Most men do not like to hear of a man abusing a woman. That makes them very upset. Other men think it's okay because it makes them feel like they are a man. I have 2 brothers, and my oldest brother raped me when I was a child. I told my youngest brother about what he did to me, he got very upset at him. He never knew after all these years, and he was quite surprised. I cried to him and he cried, and I began to explain how I have held on to this for so many years. I described the pain I felt and the helplessness. He also told me that I didn't deserve that and I was a brave woman to have dealt with this pain for so many years. He told me to go on with my life, and leave my other brother alone. He told me not to let him destroy me because he is a sick and dangerous man. His mind is very sick; he needs help in a lot of ways. My brother was very upset at him for what he did to me. He felt that I shouldn't have allowed him to be in my life and to let something that bad happen to me. I was an innocent child, and I didn't deserve that abuse. No one does, and I shouldn't feel any blame. I can't take the blame for my brother's actions. At some point when it's a family member, you learn to trust that person not thinking that they will become a predator. A family member is someone who is there for you and won't harm you in any kind of way. The encouraging words that my brother gave me lifted my spirits. Encouraging words from others helped me also. I'm writing this book because someone out there whether it's a woman or a man has been through what I've been through. By telling my story, I can encourage an individual to go get help, talk to someone and know that they are not alone. I have been through all types of abuse. I have been psychologically abused at my job. My supervisor was always nasty to me. I always call in the morning to see where I am working. He often sends me to areas that are less desirable, and he is very disrespectful to me on the phone. He doesn't use a pleasant tone of voice when I am talking to him. I still try to treat him nicely and pray for him that things will get better. Many women have dealt with men that have a drug problem. When a person is on some kind a drug, the drug begins to take control of their mind and it makes them do and say things. It often makes a person violent and it can lead to someone's death. I experienced it and often told myself that I didn't' want to be around anyone with that kind of problem. Sometimes I used to ask myself how did I get myself into this bad relationship. It wasn't a healthy relationship and I could have done something about it before it started to happen. But still it took time and I got out that relationship and I'm very happy to tell about it. I'm now ready to take control of my life and move on with my life. I'm putting all that abuse behind me and starting a new beginning. I'm now full of life and ready to get out there and enjoy it. I believe one day God is going to send me someone that respects me and will enjoy life with me. I won't look back. I will only look forward. Maybe, I will touch a woman's life when she reads my book, and she will take the time to understand what I'm trying to tell every woman who has been abused. Abuse is wrong and it's not to be tolerated. Women were not put on this earth to be abused by anyone. We are special and deserve to be treated like women should. This book goes out to all women who think they can't get out of the relationship. You can if you really want to. Try it out; you never know what will happen until you try something. Contact me and I will help you as much as I can. I will enjoy talking with you. I will let you lean on my shoulder. We both will cry on each other's shoulder. I will give you the best advice to protect yourself. I don't mind helping you because somebody had to help me also. Remember stay away from the abusive person because you never know what may happen. Often times these type of people are ashamed of themselves and don't want anybody to know that they are abusers. Abusers can get help also, if they want to change. I asked my abuser to go and get help with me but he refused to go. He finally told me that he began drinking at the age of 14. Now he is an older man and still drinking. I told him that if he didn't stop drinking it was going to destroy him. I think he likes the way he is because he enjoys having control of women. He abuses all the women he dates. I have seen this man turn into another person when he is mad and upset. When he is mad, he will say anything to try to hurt the woman. Therefore, I really don't feel like being bothered with another man right now. I am trying to get over this relationship I was in during the year 2005. I enjoy my life right now. I have a routine. I go to work, workout, attend Wednesday night Bible study, relax, and go to bed. I enjoy writing books. God gave me the gift and talent to help others by writing. I am working on my second book now, which is called, "Let him go, before it's too late." Sometimes I will lie in my bed at night writing my thoughts. I enjoy typing on the computer. It keeps me busy. If I am busy all the time, I won't think about how badly this man treated me. I am not in a hurry to get back into another relationship. I am trying to reach my goals of becoming successful in life. I am trying to get over the feeling of being abused all these years. You just don't know what this man put me through. I hope this book will help other readers with their situations because domestic violence is a critical issue for women. Even while they are dating, they need to understand that violence is very serious and should never be allowed. I just want women to think about their life. Life is precious. You only get one life and you can always find another man. Now I have learned to look deeply before I leap. I don't want to make that same mistake again. I would like to tell other women to be sure and interview men before they start dating them to see what kind of man they really are. Also be sure to check him out before you decide to date him. If you don't look deeply before you leap, later you will regret it. Before you start dating, read my book and listen to my advice. I wrote this book because I want to let other women know how dangerous it is being in a domestic violence relationship. Being in a violent relationship can cause so much damage in a person's life. Just look at the signs such as cursing, yelling, slapping, hitting, sexual abuse and choking. These are signs of an abusive relationship. If you believe you are in a domestic violence relationship, you need to get help immediately, and report him to the authorities. Women who are going through abusive relationships often times isolate themselves from others because they are ashamed and don't want anybody to know of the abuse. Domestic violence destroys your home and family. No women deserve to be abused. It is not the victim's fault that they are being abused. Domestic violence is a violent confrontation between family and relationships in the household. Domestic violence also involves physical harm, sexual assault and mental. Some abusers like to control their victims because they think they are weak. In my opinion, I feel like if your partner is controlling you, don't hesitate to let him go. Please don't ignore his behavior because this is serious. This is learned behavior often times coming from their childhood. Domestic violence hurts all family members. When a person is abused he or she eventually loses their trust and respect for the sex of the abuser. Every one has the right to feel safe in her home. Domestic violence is not a disagreement it is a pattern of bad behavior used by one partner to establish and maintain power and control over the other person. The behavior can be frequent for a long period of time. The abuser is the one who is responsible for the domestic violence and should be the one who is willing to change. Don't wait until you and the ones you love get hurt. Remember, you are not alone. Consider getting some help for yourself. Don't be silent about it, talk to someone. Often times the abuser suffers from emotional problems and mental issues. Sometimes abusers may have some problems growing up as a child. Abusers sometimes feel like they are ashamed of themselves and feel guilty about what they had done. I suffered from very deep depression. I went to counseling for help. Sometimes the memory of the abuse burdens me so deeply that it bothers me to know that someone else is suffering from domestic violence also. Some people learn how to forgive, but others my carry on with the pain. Preventing sexual abuse is very important. You body is your own and you have the right to say no. Your body belongs to you and you only. Remember the abuse is never your fault. When you first meet someone, they act nice, kind, and caring; however, as soon as you begin trusting them with your heart, they change on you. When a woman has been abused for so many years, she will never be the same. When I was abused, I isolated myself from people. It was very hard for me to believe I allowed myself to go through this type of lifestyle. I blamed myself for letting this happen to me. I should have been careful and realized something was wrong. Abusers like to fuss and fight all the time. They are cruel to people and very dangerous. They will hurt you if you don't stay out of their way. I also read up on alcoholic abusers. They are mentally strained. Often at times, the abusing starts in their childhood. Whether it's a close relative or a close friend, the abuse can occur at anytime. Alcohol can play a part in the abuse and abandonment can also take place. All of this can take part in an abuser's life and can affect the innocent person. They can grow up thinking it's okay to hurt people. They often drink a lot. They stay depressed, and they are dangerous to themselves and other people as well. My abuser physically attacked me in my own home. From the attack I became unconscious. When I awoke I noticed I had bruises all around my arm and back. Upon waking up from the attack, I was still feeling disoriented. I was quite surprised that he did this to me. I cried and prayed that God would give me the strength to leave this man. He kept apologizing to me, and he didn't remember what he did to me. He thought that I was making the attack up. But I still stayed in the relationship even though he did all of this. I really believed he was sorry for what he did. I would keep telling myself that it won't happen again and making excuses for what he did. When I first met this man, many people told me about the kind of man he was and the life he lived. He used to abuse other women in his past before he met me. They often told me that I was too classy of a woman to be with a man like that. You deserve better! People thought something was wrong with me and felt like I had a problem. When we went out in public, people would stare and whisper about us. My daughter didn't care for the man. She would tell me all the time to stay away from him and get my self together because that wasn't me. She was right in so many ways. My self-esteem was low, and I believed he was a good man. Being in a relationship with a man is what made me feel good. I haven't been in a relationship for many years. I got tired of being lonely and I needed a companion. They told me to stay away from him because he will hurt me. One of his family members also told me things about him, and he believed the abuse would take place and that I would see. I didn't listen to him or anybody else. I thought everyone was against our relationship, and he was right for me. But everything that was told to me came to past. I knew at that moment I needed to break free of him and get out the relationship before someone got hurt. I was afraid of him—afraid of him or what he might do to my family. When I did break free from the relationship, I started to research how the abusers think and why they abuse others. I went to the library and read a book on alcohol abuse. I started to understand the things that happened to me and to realize that I wasn't the blame for it. Some of the things I read about in the book had happen to me. One thing that the book explained that caught my eye is that you should never fight your abuser back. They will get angry and they can seriously hurt you. I did fight my abuser back because I was afraid of the harm he could do to me. Fighting him led to increased physical abuse, yet I continued to stay in the relationship. I pictured myself in the book as I was reading. In the book, it mentioned some things that were familiar. I start to remember how cruel he was to me. He didn't care about me or himself. He wanted to use me and control me at all times. He didn't want me to go around other people. He wanted me all to himself so he could argue and fight, but I thank God that I got out that relationship. I'm so grateful for my friends and family and the prayers. I feel good about myself. I think back and realize I could have lost my life and see everything that I have accomplished. I am now in college working on my degree. I attend Grand Canyon University. I am working toward my Bachelor degree in Psychology. I will graduate in 2010, and after that I plan to go back and get my masters. I will work toward my master's degree. I am a happy woman. I wrote this book because I wanted to help women that are in abusive relationships. Writing this book has taught me that situations can change; you just have to be willing to be the one to make the first step to change. I believe I have the gift of writing so I can help others through my writing. I hope this book will be a great help to you.

Every word that I wrote in this book is true. My next book that I plan to write will be, "Women let him go, before it's too late. The second book will be better than this one. This book has impacted my life a lot. Domestic violence is a topic that should be addressed by everyone. I wrote this book to talk about how domestic violence has impacted my life, and I hope that another young lady can read it and gain some type of important information from it. We should support those women who are determined to break away from their domestic violence relationships. I would like to see these women move on with their lives and don't look back. Often times women would leave their abusive mate and then eventually take him back. Some women get weak because they are so in love, and they get lonely. They feel like he is the only man out there that will be with them. Why would you want to go back to a bad relationship? I don't believe a real woman would go back to her abuser. Women who go back to their abuser should go get some counseling. I learned not to go back to my abuser, and I stayed away from him. I am going forward with my life because I know that there is something out there better for me. I don't think any women deserve to be treated like a punching bag. She deserves to be treated with respect and dignity. Abuse situations should be avoided. There is no excuse for domestic violence. I put a stop to my abuser so I know you can also. I can remember one day I was in church, and I began to cry and cry. I couldn't stop. There was a young lady who came to me and asked me what was wrong. I wouldn't tell her what's wrong because I was too embarrassed and ashamed. She said to me, "I will pray for you and hope things get better for you." "Hold your head up and quit looking sad." Her words of wisdom really influenced me to get out that bad relationship. After that lady said those words to me, I started to attend church more. Something about being in church made me feel better about myself. When I was dating this man, I started not to attend church as I used to. I stayed home with this man and I just felt at the time that I was less than a person. Often at times I felt like I was getting what I deserved, and it was okay. I thought that if I could be a better person I would not be abused or mistreated by anyone. An abuser can prey on a woman. He feels a weak personality who won't stand up for herself. I just realized he had no power over me. I can stand up for myself! I have all the power in me through God. I'm more determined today that I will never be in an abusive relationship. I'm now saved and attend church regularly. I am now studying to be a counselor so that I can help others to break the chains that are enslaving our women. I hope that young women and teenagers who find themselves in similar situations can gain some kind of information from this book. I want to take a stand against domestic violence toward women. Finally I got over what this man did to me. Now I am happy and ready for a change. I took authority over my life and I left him. I was so tired of being stressed out. I have gotten over my bad experience. Now I am waiting for God to send me the right man for me. I got my joy back. I have now closed that chapter of my life and I am ready to help other women close that chapter also. I would like to end this book by saying that I cried my last tear yesterday about all that I have gone through with this man. I still have joy and I thank God that I made it. If you have been a victim of abuse, I want to leave you with these words coming from Mrs. Ratliff. Make this your motto, "I am trying to get over my ex so that I can get my next." May God bless you.

By: Mrs. Willie Bell Ratliff

ACKNOWLEDGMENTS

First, I would like to thank the Lord, the One who opened up my knowledge to write this book, 'Women,' get out of the domestic violence relationship. My greatest love goes out to my two daughters, who have tremendously supported me in my efforts. Next, I want to express my love to my two sisters. They are ministers and have prayed earnestly that God will help me to move on with my life. I also want to extend a special thanks to a good friend of mine. She teaches Bible History in a couple of Hamilton County Schools, and has tried to help me in my efforts.

I would like to express my appreciation to the counselor and therapist who spent time listening to my problems and sharing their insight and thoughts with me. My thanks go out to all of the teenagers who shared their lives with me. Being able to cry on each other's shoulder and hug one another was helpful for us all. My gratitude goes out to a special person who means the world to me. That is my aunt. She raised me when my mother passed. She means so much to me that I could never express. She was a great help to me and to my brother. Without her help, I would not be where I am today. I'll never forget her and all that she did for me. She will always have a special place in my heart.

There will also always be a special place in my heart for my mother, Mary Jean Roberson. She died giving me birth. My mother deserves a special endorsement. She is the one I will always love.

LaVergne, TN USA
25 September 2009
159065LV00003B/124/P